Matchstick Mini loves Halloween
By Edel Malone

Original concept created, illustrated, and written by Edel Malone. I'm sure you will love these books as much as I do. I know you will enjoy making lasting memories with your child moving forward in all stages of their lives by encouraging your child to tell you what's on their mind throughout their lifetime. Asking questions is the way forward. Check out some of the other Matchstick Mini books. Sizes and colors may vary for printed books.

D1465240

The Matchstick Mini books are designed to encourage your child to open up and talk about what is on their mind from an early age. The topics covered are related to young children to encourage good communication techniques carrying on into each stage of their lives, keeping safety and values in mind.

OTHER BOOKS FROM MATCHSTICK MINI

Matchstick Mini and safety

Matchstick Mini and others

Matchstick Mini has fun

Matchstick Mini and school

Matchstick Mini is very good

Matchstick Mini is healthy

Matchstick Mini and grief

Matchstick Mini loves Halloween, and he loves decorating the house with pretend spiders, spider webs, and ghosts. Matchstick Mini knows they are not real and has lots of fun decorating his home for Halloween. Matchstick Mini knows Halloween is not scary. It is just for fun.

Matchstick Mini loves when he gets a pumpkin for Halloween, and he likes helping an adult to carve a scary face onto it. Matchstick Mini thinks pumpkins are cool, and he lets an adult light the candle to put inside the pumpkin.

Matchstick Mini loves going to school when it is Halloween for the Halloween party and has some sweets and treats. Matchstick Mini won't eat too many sweets because he knows too many sweets are bad for him and only eats them on special occasions.

When Matchstick Mini is in school, he makes Halloween decorations. Matchstick Mini makes a paper plate with a spider on it to bring home and some black spiders too. Matchstick Mini uses his spider decoration to decorate his house.

Matchstick Mini dresses up as a superhero for the school Halloween party. Matchstick Mini loves to dress up, and his favorite costume is his superhero costume. Matchstick Mini thinks he is a real superhero with superhero powers. Matchstick Mini believes fruit and vegetables and water give him superpowers and lots of energy.

Matchstick Mini loves looking at all the different costumes, and he thinks Halloween is fun. Matchstick Mini's sister loves to dress up as a princess, and she loves to wear her crown. Matchstick Mini tells his sister she looks very pretty, and this makes his sister happy. Matchstick Mini knows it is nice to say nice things to other people.

Matchstick Mini loves to look at the fireworks on Halloween night, and he thinks they look fantastic. Matchstick Mini won't touch the fireworks until he is older, and he lets an adult do them. Matchstick Mini knows fireworks can be dangerous. Matchstick Mini thinks all the different colored fireworks look amazing, and he enjoys watching them for ages. Do you know that you should not touch fireworks like Matchstick Mini?

Matchstick Mini knows that some small children are afraid of the noise the fireworks make. When the fireworks go off, Matchstick Mini tells the little children not to be scared because it is okay, and it is only loud noise. Matchstick Mini's little sister tells them to look at how pretty they are and tells them to forget about the noise. Are you afraid of the loud noise that fireworks make?

Matchstick Mini knows that cats and dogs are afraid of the noise that fireworks make too, he knows the noise of the fireworks makes some animals scared. So Matchstick Mini always brings his dog and cat into his house when the fireworks are going off. Matchstick Mini does not want them to be scared. Even though he knows that you should not be afraid of loud noises, he understands that some small children and animals are so scared of the noise they make.

Matchstick Mini loves going to the bonfire too, and he only goes when an adult is with him. Matchstick Mini likes to look at the bonfire, and he knows that he should not stand near the bonfire because it is scorching hot, and you could get burnt. Matchstick Mini always stays near an adult and holds an adult's hand so he won't get lost. Matchstick Mini is very clever.

Matchstick Mini loves to go trick or treating, and he always goes with an adult. Matchstick Mini's little sister and his friends go too. Matchstick Mini likes to knock on the doors or ring the doorbell and say trick or treat, and he thinks trick or treating is lots of fun because you get to chat with lots of people. No one knocks at the houses with no decorations and no lights on because people may not be in, or some people may not like answering the door because they are sick.

When Matchstick Mini knocks on the doors and says trick or treats, people open the door and give him fruit or sweets. Matchstick Mini has lovely manners and says thank you and looks forward to going to the next house. Do you have lovely manners like Matchstick Mini? Some children are shy and don't want to talk and that's okay too.

When Matchstick Mini gets home, he looks into his bag to see what is in it. Matchstick Mini is pleased with all his sweets and treats. Matchstick Mini won't eat all his sweets in one day because that would be silly and make him feel sick. Matchstick Mini eats his sweets over the next few days, and he shares them with everyone at home.

Matchstick Mini loves to play Halloween games when he gets home from trick or treating. One of the games he plays is apple bobbing. Matchstick Mini puts his face into the basin of water with apples in it. Matchstick Mini tries to get one of the apples out without using his hands, he has great fun, and everyone thinks it is hilarious. Everyone takes turns with the apple bobbing, and Halloween is fun.

Printed in Great Britain
by Amazon